Handy New Hampshire Genealogy Handbook

By Gary L. Morris

©2015 Gary L. Morris

ISBN-13: 978-1506148601

ISBN-10: 1506148603

Table of Contents

About Genealogical Research in New Hampshire

New Hampshire has one of the oldest histories in the United States, and as such is rich in genealogical materials. Records have been generated since 1640, newspapers published from the mid-eighteenth century, and the oral histories of its native inhabitants passed on for thousands of years. As you can imagine there is a wealth of genealogical resources in New Hampshire, what we aim to do in this guide is to tell you:

1. What They are
2. Where to Find Them
3. How to Use Them

These valuable resources can be found both online and off, so we'll introduce you to some online databases and indexes, as well as the many brick-and-mortar repositories, societies and organizations that will help with your genealogical research in New Hampshire. In order to give you a more comprehensive understanding of these records, we'll also give you a brief history of "The Granite State", a state that has needed its inhabitants to be of sturdy build and strong character as its modern nickname suggests.

A Brief History of New Hampshire

New Hampshire is unique among the early colonies, as it was not founded by those seeking to escape religious persecution. Rather Captain John Mason, in alliance with several unknown associates, commissioned a Scotsman by the name of David Thompson along with two Englishmen named Thomas and Edward Hilton, along with a group of others to establish a fishing colony on the Piscataqua River. Colonies were established at what are now the towns of Rye and Dover in 1623, and so begun a long and colorful history.

A community of "towns" was erected under guidance from the English government, and the region was established as a "royal province" in 1679. John Cutt was elected as president, and the population governed and organized as much like England as was possible. New Hampshire remained a "royal province" until 1698 when it fell under the jurisdiction of Massachusetts and its Governor Joseph Dudley, and continued as such until 1741.

New Hampshire remained under English sovereignty until the Revolutionary War. In 1774, citizens of New Hampshire had signaled their devotion to the Revolution by stealing guns and powder from Fort William. They went on to fight in the Battle of Bunker Hill, where they made up the majority of the revolutionary force. Three citizens of New Hampshire would eventually sign the American Declaration of Independence; Mathew Thornton, Josiah Bartlett, and William Whipple.

New Hampshire was the first state to declare its independence and to adopt its own constitution, before becoming the deciding state in accepting the National Constitution proclaiming America a republic; New Hampshire had never known any other form of government. Many subsequent events have contributed to New Hampshire's history, and as the first ever state library was established there, its genealogical value can not be understated.

Important Genealogical Dates in New Hampshire History

- **1623 – 1638** - The first settlements were established in New Hampshire at Dover, Plymouth, Hampton and Exeter by religious dissenters, fishermen and traders.
- **1641 -1679** - During this period all settlements in New Hampshire fell under the jurisdiction of Massachusetts, and consequently most of the records from this period are held in Massachusetts at the State Archives and similar institutions.
- **1679** -New Hampshire separated from Massachusetts.
- **1739 – 1741** -Massachusetts/New Hampshire boundary dispute finally settled.
- **1754 – 1763** - An influx of soldiers during the French and Indian War opened the way for many new settlements to be established in New Hampshire
- **1764** - First major boundary changed as the west bank of the Connecticut River was declared as New Hampshire's western boundary.
- **1755 – 1783** - Many settlers from New Hampshire fought and killed during the Revolutionary War
- **1788** -New Hampshire becomes the ninth state after ratifying the US Constitution.
- **1819** - With the passing of the Toleration Act, New Hampshire residents were freed from the paying of compulsory taxes to any church.
- **1842** - New Hampshire's boundary with Quebec was settled, and consequently many French Canadians began crossing the border to work in New Hampshire's textile mills and shoe factories.
- **1861 – 1865** -Nearly forty thousand New Hampshire residents fought and killed during Civil war
- **1898** - Spanish American War involving nearly 300,000 Americans sees 1,358 New Hampshire soldiers fighting in Cuba and the Philippines.
- **1917 – 1918**: Many men from New Hampshire aged 18 – 45 register with the Selective Service during World War 1.

- **1930's -** The great Depression caused many of New Hampshire's factories to close, and many of the smaller farms to be shut down and abandoned. Many New Hampshire families moved to the cities.
- **1940 – 1945 -** New Hampshire men and women fight and die in the Second World War.
- **1950 – 1953 =** New Hampshire men and women fight in Korean War; approximately 150 New Hampshire soldiers killed or missing in action.
- **1964 – 1972 -** New Hampshire men and women fight in Vietnam War; 227 New Hampshire residents killed or missing in action.

Common New Hampshire Genealogical Issues and Resources to Overcome Them

Boundary Changes: A common obstacle when researching New Hampshire ancestors are historical boundary changes. One can be searching for an ancestor's record in one county when in fact it is stored in a different one due to historical county boundary changes. The **Atlas of Historical County Boundaries** can help you to overcome that problem. It provides a chronological listing of every boundary change that has occurred in the history of New Hampshire.

Atlas of Historical County Boundaries:
http://publications.newberry.org/ahcbp/documents/NH_Consolidated_Chronology.htm#Consolidated_Chronology

Name Changes: Surname changes, variations, and misspellings can complicate genealogical research. It is important to check all spelling variations. Soundex, a program that indexes names by sound, is a useful first step, but you can't rely on it completely as some name variations result in different Soundex codes. The surnames could be different, but the first name may be different too. You can also find records filed under initials, middle names, and nicknames as well, so you will need to **get creative with surname variations** and spellings in order to cover all the possibilities. For help with surname variations read our instructional article on **How to Use Soundex**.

get creative with surname variations:
http://obituarieshelp.org/blog/?p=634

How to Use Soundex: http://obituarieshelp.org/blog/?p=505

New Hampshire Genealogical Organizations and Archives

Genealogical resources include not only records, but the organizations that house them, or can direct you to them. These institutions include: *Archives, Libraries, Genealogical Societies, Family History Centers, Universities, Churches, and Museums.*

Archives

New Hampshire State Archives - a genealogist's paradise hosting a wealth of records ranging from Census Reports, Probate Records, Land Records, Military records, and Naturalization Records to Paupers indices and more

Archives and Records Management
N.H. Department of State
71 South Fruit Street
Concord, NH 03301
Tel: 603-271-2236
Fax: 603-271-2272
Email: archives@sos.nh.gov

New Hampshire State Archives:
http://sos.nh.gov/Arch_Rec_Mgmt.aspx

N.H. Vital Records Administration (formerly N.H. Bureau of Vital Records) - repository for Birth, Death, Marriage and Divorce records in the state from colonial era to 1948.

New Hampshire Vital Records Administration
71 South Fruit Street
Concord, NH 03301
Tel: 603-271-2236
Fax: 603-271-2272
Email: archives@sos.nh.gov

N.H. Vital Records Administration:
http://www.sos.nh.gov/vitalrecords/FAQ.html

Massachusetts State Archives – Vital records, military records, passenger lists, judicial records, and the "archive collection" - an important source of records for early Massachusetts, Maine, and New Hampshire families.

Massachusetts State Archives:
http://www.sec.state.ma.us/arc/arcgen/genidx.htm

New Hampshire State Library - maintains an extensive collection of 2400 published family histories for New Hampshire and the rest of New England as well as annual town reports, town and county histories, Federal census records, city and county directories, military indexes up to 1900, historical newspapers collection (microfilm)

New Hampshire State Library
20 Park Street
Concord, NH 03301
603-271-2144
Tel: (603) 271-2144 or 603-271-22

New Hampshire State Library: https://www.nh.gov/nhsl/

Manchester New Hampshire City Library - collection contains city and town histories, biographies, Manchester history, and genealogies of prominent New Hampshire families.

Manchester City Library
405 Pine St.
Manchester, NH o3104
Tel. - 603 624-6550
Email: via online contact form

Manchester New Hampshire City Library:
http://www.manchester.lib.nh.us/

The University of New Hampshire - holds a wealth of valuable genealogical material such as an impressive digital collection of old newspapers, Civil War Records (personal papers, muster rolls, regimental histories and soldier's letters) as well as the New Hampshire Genealogical Record, an historical genealogy magazine from the early 20th century (1904 -1909), and annual reports for individual towns dating from 1866, including journals and provincial papers.

University of New Hampshire
105 Main Street,
Durham, NH 03824
Tel: 603) 862-1234

The University of New Hampshire: http://www.unh.edu/

Sullivan Public Library Archive – Town records, school records and memorabilia, newspaper clippings, photographs, town clerk records, religious records, cemetery records, deeds, manuscripts.

Sullivan Public Library Archive:
http://www.ci.sullivan.nh.us/content/library/library-archives

New Hampshire Genealogical and Historical Societies

Genealogical and historical societies have access to extensive catalogues of genealogical data. They are also able to offer expert guidance for genealogical researchers. Many members are professional genealogists who are most willing to share their expertise in finding ancestors.

New Hampshire Historical Society - Another resource located in Concord, the N.H. Historical Society's library boasts the finest collection of printed, manuscript, and historical photographs relating to New Hampshire history that you'll find anywhere. Their incredible manuscript collection includes the personal papers of many historically notable individuals such as; Josiah Bartlett who signed the American Declaration of Independence, Mary Baker eddy the founder of Christian Science, and the famous orator Daniel Webster. You will also find; account books, indentures, diaries, business records, organizational and corporate records relating to farmers, shopkeepers, craftsmen, agricultural, medical, religious, social, cultural, and industrial groups.

Museum
6 Eagle Square
Concord, NH 03301
Tel: 603-228-6688

Library
30 Park Street
Concord, NH 03301
Tel:603-228-6688

New Hampshire Historical Society: https://www.nhhistory.org/

American – Canadian Genealogical Society (ACGS) - maintains the biggest resource facility for French-Canadian research in the United States of America. Their primary resources are Parish records which cover the provinces of Quebec, New Brunswick, and Ontario in Canada, as well as the states of Maine, New Hampshire, Rhode Island, and Massachusetts in the U.S. They also have vital records for New Hampshire up to 1900.

American-Canadian Genealogical Society
P.O. Box 6478
Manchester, NH   03108-6478
Tel: 603-622-1554
Email: ACGS@acgs.org

American – Canadian Genealogical Society: http://www.acgs.org/

New England Historic Genealogical Society - Founded in 1758, this organization has searchable online databases of genealogical records from all over New England. Some of the records you can search here particular to New Hampshire are; Marriage records, Doctors personal records of births 1807-1857, Church Records, Mortality Bills (Deaths from 1708-1802), Vital Records from 1686-1850, Town records, and Tax lists.

New England Historic Genealogical Society
99 - 101 Newbury Street
Boston, Massachusetts 02116
Tel: 617-536-5740

New England Historic Genealogical Society:
http://www.americanancestors.org/home.html

Historical Society of Cheshire County – The Wright Room research library here contains over 3,000 volumes on New England towns, counties, and family histories, complete with a comprehensive and current collection of CD ROMs related to genealogy, vital records, and military records

Historical Society of Cheshire County; http://www.hsccnh.org/

Wolfeboro Historical Society – Local histories, genealogies, historical photos, town reports, personal notes

Wolfeboro Historical Society;
http://www.wolfeborohistoricalsociety.org/

New Hampshire Family History Centers

The Family History Centers run by the LDS Church offer free access to billions of genealogical records for free to the general public. They also provide classes on genealogy and one-on-one assistance to inexperienced family historians. At the online directory for **LDS Family History Centers** you will find Addresses and contact information for LDS Family History Centers in New Hampshire

LDS Family History Centers:
http://www.familysearch.org/eng/library/FHC/frameset_fhc.asp

Additional New Hampshire Genealogical Resources

New Hampshire Mailing Lists

Mailing lists are internet based facilities that use email to distribute a single message to all who subscribe to it. When information on a particular surname, new records, or any other important genealogy information related to the mailing list topic becomes available, the subscribers are alerted to it. Joining a mailing list is an excellent way to stay up to date on New Hampshire genealogy research topics. Rootsweb have an extensive listing of **New Hampshire Mailing Lists** on a variety of topics.

New Hampshire Mailing Lists:
http://lists.rootsweb.ancestry.com/index/usa/NH/misc.html

New Hampshire Message Boards

A message board is another internet based facility where people can post questions about a specific genealogy topic and have it answered by other genealogists. If you have questions about a surname, record type, or research topic, you can post your question and other researchers and genealogists will help you with the answer. You must make sure to check back regularly, as the answers are not emailed to you. The message boards at the **New Hampshire Genealogy Forum** are completely free to use.

New Hampshire Genealogy Forum:
http://genforum.genealogy.com/nh/

Newspapers and Periodicals

The **NH Index** is a database of article citations from several New Hampshire newspapers and magazines. The newspapers and periodicals in NH Index are NOT indexed cover to cover. Only citations to articles pertaining to state issues, culture and history are included in this index. Also, New Hampshire Index does not include the full text of the articles, only the citation to the articles.

NH Index:
http://www.nh.gov/nhsl/services/public/newspaper_content.html

New Hampshire Newspaper Project

Completed in the early 1990s, the NH Newspaper Project undertook to microfilm newspapers published in New Hampshire which were deemed critical for preservation based on the physical condition of the paper. This work was completed with a grant from the National Endowment for the Humanities as part of the United States Newspaper Project.

New Hampshire Newspaper Project:
http://www.nh.gov/nhsl/nhais/newspaper_project.html

New Hampshire Newspapers Online

Several New Hampshire newspapers are available on the internet.

New Hampshire Newspapers Online:
http://www.nh.gov/nhnews/index.html

NH Historical Newspapers on Microfilm

An index to the New Hampshire State Library's collection of statewide newspapers.

NH Historical Newspapers on Microfilm:
http://stats.library.state.nh.us/dbtw-wpd/nhpaper/nhpaper.html

New Hampshire City and County Directories

Although local historical and genealogical societies may prove the best resources for these valuable genealogical materials, you can also find them at the following institutions.

The **Library of Congress Reading Room** - has a host of New Hampshire City Directories on microfilm. A full listing of the cities and the dates for which they have records can be viewed on their website.

Library of Congress Reading Room link to;
http://www.loc.gov/rr/microform/uscity/nh.html

New Hampshire Historical Directories - listing links you to where the directories may be found online, some for free and others involving payment.

New Hampshire Historical Directories link to:
http://sites.google.com/site/onlinedirectorysite/Home/usa/nh

The best source for both online and online research is the **New Hampshire State Library**. They have an extensive collection of city and town directories as well as other historical data that can be viewed online in high quality resolution.

New Hampshire State Library link to;
http://www.nh.gov/nhsl/services/public/genealogy.html

Historical New Hampshire Maps and Gazetteers

Maps are necessary to genealogical research. They help us to locate landmarks, towns, cities, parishes, states, provinces, waterways and roads and streets. They also help us to determine when and where boundary changes might have taken place, and give us a visualization of the area we're researching in. For locating place names, a gazetteer is the best possible resource for any genealogist. Gazetteers are also sometimes called "place name dictionaries", and can help you to locate the area in which you need to conduct research. Below are links to the maps and gazetteers for research in New Hampshire.

Peabody GNIS Service – New Hampshire: http://peabody.research.yale.edu/cgi-bin/Query.GNIS?ST=New%20Hampshire&SU=1

1985 U.S. Atlas: http://www.livgenmi.com/1895/NH/

New Hampshire Hometown Locator: http://newhampshire.hometownlocator.com/

New Hampshire Genealogical Records

Birth, Death and Marriage Records

In the state of New Hampshire, you can obtain BDM certificates (birth, death, and marriage) from either the city or town clerk, or the **NH Vital Records Administration**. Records date back to 1640.

NH Vital Records Administration;
http://www.sos.nh.gov/vitalrecords/ELIGIBILITY.html

Divorce Records

Divorce records in New Hampshire are held on microfilm at the **Department of State Division of Vital Records Administration**. The available state indexes that you can find there are:

The Bride's Index – Dating from 1640-1900, contains the names of brides, the mothers of brides and the mothers of grooms. Film Number: 0975678 ff.
Index to Divorces – lists divorces from early colonial period to 1936. Film Number: 1001323 ff.
Many county court records have been microfilmed and are also held by the Vital Records Administration. Although they contain divorce records they are not catalogued as such. Those that have been transferred to microfilm are:

Grafton County Superior court of Judicature Court Records – Records from 1774 – 1851, includes divorce cases overseen by the Grafton County Courthouse. Microfilm Number: 1763455 ff.

Grafton County Supreme Court Equity Records – 1881-1918, includes divorce records kept by both the Supreme and Superior Courts. Microfilm Number: 1763365 ff.

Department of State
Division of Vital Records Administration:
http://sos.nh.gov/vital_records.aspx

Census Reports

The Federal government conducted the first census of New Hampshire in 1790. Since then they have continued to be taken every ten years. You can access New Hampshire census reports up until 1930, most are complete except for the 1890 census which was lost in the same warehouse fire that destroyed those of other states. Every one of the New Hampshire reports has been indexed except for those of 1870 and 1910.

The **New Hampshire State Library** holds the original schedules for 1850, 1860, 1870, 1880, and has microfilm copies of those from 1800, 1810, 1820, and 1830. It also retains printed copies of the first Federal United States census taken in 1790.

New Hampshire State Library: https://www.nh.gov/nhsl/

Prior to 1790 there are enumeration lists available at the State Archives for 1732, 1744, 1767, and 1776. They can be found in the **New Hampshire Provincial and State Papers** which are housed at most libraries throughout New Hampshire. Some of the census reports are not complete.

For example the 1800 report omits the towns of Atkinson, Greenland, Hampton, Hampton Falls, Londonderry, Northampton, Pelham, Plaistow, Salem, Seabrook, Stratham, and Windham in Rockingham County, and Alton, Barnstead, Brookfield, Effingham, Gilmanton, Middleton, New Durham, Ossipee, and Tuftonboro, Wakefield, and Wolfeboro in Strafford County.

Information for the towns in Strafford County that were omitted in the 1800 report can be found in the **1798 Direct Tax List**, which contains the occupants name, and the name of the properties owner if not the same. A copy is currently held by the **Wolfeboro Historical Society**, and other copies can be found in the **State Archives**, the **State Library**, and with the **New Hampshire Historical Society**.

New Hampshire Church Records

Church records can reveal much genealogical material, and there are many to be found in New Hampshire.

An excellent comprehensive source and guide to church records in New Hampshire is the 1942 publication *Guide to Church Vital Statistics in New Hampshire*. Published by the New Hampshire Historical Records Survey, Service Division, Work Projects Administration. It is an essential guide to where specific church records can be found in the state. You can obtain a printed copy at the **New Hampshire Division of Records Management and Archives.** You can also find microfilmed copies in genealogical libraries and the **LDS Family History Centers** throughout the state.

New Hampshire Division of Records Management and Archives: http://www.sos.nh.gov/archives/about.html

LDS Family History Centers: http://www.familysearch.org/eng/library/FHC/frameset_fhc.asp

The American Baptist-Samuel Colgate Library in Rochester New York has some original records of the American Baptist Church in New Hampshire from various towns. A list of the records they have for New Hampshire can be found online in their **Archive of Original Records Directory,** scroll down to New Hampshire.

Archive of Original Records Directory: http://www.abhsarchives.org/docs/Colgate_Original.pdf

Records of the Catholic church are some of the most prized to be found in New Hampshire. The original records are maintained by the parish in which they are or were generated and requests can be made to those institutions. You can find a listing of every Catholic Church in New Hampshire at **Parishes Online**.

Parishes Online: http://www.parishesonline.com/scripts/default.asp

The Congregational church was one of the earliest to be established in New Hampshire, and joined with other Protestant faiths to form the United Church of Christ in 1957. They have an **Online Directory** which you can use to find their congregations in New Hampshire.

The **Congregational Records and Archives Library** in Boston, Massachusetts hosts a few collections from congregations in New Hampshire, and they also have an **Online Directory of Repositories in New Hampshire** where you can find Congregational records.

Congregational Records and Archives Library:
http://www.14beacon.org/

Online Directory of Repositories in New Hampshire;
http://www.uiweb.uidaho.edu/special-collections/east2.html

Local congregations are responsible for maintaining membership records, and a listing of all **Methodist Churches in New Hampshire** can help you to find the required contact information. Listings are quite comprehensive and include the name of the pastor presently presiding; street address, telephone number, email address, and website link if the congregation has one.

As a final option, **Church Angel** has a listing of many churches in New Hampshire which you can search according to town.

Methodist Churches in New Hampshire:
http://archives.umc.org/Directory/ChurchDirectory.asp?ptid=1&mid=222

Church Angel link to: http://www.churchangel.com/newhamp.htm

Holdings by Denomination

Baptist

American Baptist Churches of Vermont and New Hampshire
P.O. Box 1206
Lebanon, NH 03766
Phone: (603) 643-4201
Fax: (603) 228-6129

American Baptist Churches of Vermont and New Hampshire:
http://abcvnh.org/

American Baptist Historical Society
3001 Mercer University Dr.
Atlanta, GA 30341
Phone: (678) 547-6680

American Baptist Historical Society: http://abhsarchives.org/

Mormon Church records for New Hampshire can be found on film located at the LDS Family History Library in Salt Lake City and can be searched via the **Family History Library Catalog**

Family History Library Catalog:
https://familysearch.org/eng/Library/FHLC/frameset_fhlc.asp

Congregational

United Church of Christ, New Hampshire Conference
314 S. Main St.
Concord, NH 03301
Phone: (603) 225-6647

Older Congregational church records of congregations no longer in existence are at the **New Hampshire Historical Society**.

United Church of Christ, New Hampshire Conference:
http://www.14beacon.org/

Episcopal

The Episcopal Diocese of New Hampshire
63 Green St.
Concord, NH 03301
Phone: (603) 224-1914

The Episcopal Diocese of New Hampshire:
http://www.nhepiscopal.org/

The **New Hampshire Historical Society** has the church records of various New Hampshire Episcopalian congregations, which are held in the archives.

Methodist

United Methodist Church, Conference Office
62 Government Street
Kittery, ME 03904-1563
Phone: (207) 439-9686
Email: stmarks.me@compuserve.com

United Methodist Church, Conference Office:
http://www.umc.org/

A portion of the records of older Methodist congregations have been deposited at:

School of Theology Library
745 Commonwealth Ave.
Boston, MA 02215
Telephone: (617) 353-3034
Fax: (617) 353-3061

School of Theology Library:
http://www.bu.edu/academics/sth/school-of-theology-resources/

Presbyterian

Presbyterian Historical Society
425 Lombard St.
Philadelphia, PA 19147
Phone: (215) 627-1852

Presbyterian Historical Society: http://www.history.pcusa.org/

The **New Hampshire Historical Society** has Presbyterian records for Antrim, Bedford, Chester, Derry, Hampton, Londonderry, Pembroke, and Seabrook.

Roman Catholic

Diocese of Manchester
153 Ash Street
P.O. Box 310
Manchester, NH 03105
Phone: (603) 669-3100
Fax: (603) 669-0377

Diocese of Manchester: http://www.catholicnh.org/search-results/?q=

A number of Catholic baptismal and marriage records have been published and are held by the **New Hampshire Historical Society** and the **American-Canadian Genealogical Society.**

Society of Friends (Quakers)

Rhode Island Historical Society Library
121 Hope St.
Providence, RI 02906
Phone: (401) 331-8575

Rhode Island Historical Society Library: http://www.rihs.org/

New Hampshire Military Records

Because of its revolutionary past, many military records regarding New Hampshire and those who served in both National Forces and State Militias can be found. Because there are so many, we'll categorize them by conflict to make it easier for you to locate the ones that might serve you best. These records date from the 1600's up until the Vietnam conflict, identify persons who either served in the military or who were eligible for military service.

Colonial Military Records

Very early military records regarding New Hampshire may be found in the New Hampshire Provincial and State Papers found in most libraries or in the LDS Family History Centers throughout the State. The papers also include information on those who served in the French and Indian Wars between 1754 and 1763. You can also find these records in the New Hampshire State Archives – ask to view the Adjutant General's Report Vol. ii, 1866.

Revolutionary War Records

Revolutionary War records can be divided into two categories - those for *Patriots* and those for *Loyalists* who remained loyal to England during the conflict. They date from 1775 – 1783 and can be found in several locations.

Patriots

A major source for records of those who were patriots during the Revolutionary War can be found in the *Revolutionary War Rolls 1775–1783* from the United States War Department held in the National Archives. They are microfilmed compilations of the records of individual soldiers. The New Hampshire records can be found in films 830322-830333 in the LDS Family history Centers as well. The New Hampshire Historical Society has a 71 volume index of names for the New Hampshire soldiers who received pensions, as well as a card index to revolutionary War Rolls.

The **Daughters of the American Revolution (DAR)** have a Free Lookup Message Board where volunteers will check to see if your ancestor is listed in the DAR Patriot Index.

Daughters of the American Revolution Lookup Board;
http://boards.rootsweb.com/topics.organizations.dar/mb.ashx

A history of New Hampshire women patriots is give at **SeaCoastNH.com**, where many names are mentioned along with dates and addresses.

SeaCoastNH.com: http://seacoastnh.com/framers/women.html

Loyalists

The **Loyalist Collection** held by the Harriet Irving Library at the University of New Brunswick in Canada is valuable source of Loyalist records. The collection includes Loyalist related primary source material regarding British, Canadian, and Colonial American activity during the American revolutionary War. Such sources include; Official documents and military correspondence, journals, maps, muster rolls, diaries, Carleton's Loyalist Index, payment lists, settlement lists, and pensions lists.

Loyalist Collection;
http://www.lib.unb.ca/collections/loyalist/browse.php?cmd=oneSection&value=Military

War of 1812

The War of 1812 was a conflict brought on by trade restrictions imposed on the Americans by the British and their support of the Indian tribes against the new colonists. The bulk of records for this conflict can be found in the **US National Archives** in Washington D.C., but there are some accessible online records as well.

The **1840 Census of Pensioners Revolutionary or Military Services** contains the names of pensioners and widows who were receiving military pensions in New Hampshire at that time. This would have included veterans of the War of 1812 or their surviving spouse. The listing contains the name of the pensioner, as well as the name of the head of the household in which they resided, along with the pensioners name and place of residence.

1840 Census of Pensioners Revolutionary or Military Services: http://www.us-roots.org/colonialamerica/census/1840/1840nh_a.html

A Transcript of the Pension List of the United States for 1813 contains 117 names of military pensioners from New Hampshire, and there are names of some New Hampshire prisoners of war who died in the British Prison at Dartmoor at the **Dartmoor Prison Cemetery Project**.

Dartmoor Prison Cemetery Project: http://my.execpc.com/~sril/dartmoor/1812apow.htm

Civil War Records

New Hampshire soldiers played a major role in the success of the Union forces during the Civil War. Almost 40,000 men from New Hampshire served in various regiments during the four year period, and as such many records were created for them. A great online resource for New Hampshire Civil War records is the **Civil War Soldiers and Sailors System**, a completely free search engine run by the National Park Service that allows you to search 6.3 million soldier records by name, unit, state or function.

Civil War Soldiers and Sailors System; http://www.civilwar.nps.gov/cwss/soldiers.cfm

20th Century Records

The **US National Archives** holds many records from the two World Wars as well as the Korean and Vietnam Wars. They range from casualty lists to records of combat operations, medal awards, official personnel files, enlistment and draft records, unit patrol records, and many historical photographs. Records only become available to the public 62 years after the end of a person's service, so more recent records may not be available.

US National Archives: http://www.archives.gov/research/military/

When ordering copies of records from the National Archives, be aware that only a veteran or next of kin (surviving spouse, father, mother, sister, brother, daughter, or son) can receive copies, but generally there is no fee involved. Records can be ordered online, by fax, or by mail

New Hampshire Cemetery Records

New Hampshire Tombstone Inscription Project – database of records from the 18th and 19th centuries; includes major cemeteries, as well as smaller family plots with only one headstone remaining.
.
New Hampshire Tombstone Inscription Project:
http://www.usgwtombstones.org/newhamp/newhamp.html

A Very Grave Matter - This website features a wealth of photos and historical information of cemeteries and gravestones in southern New Hampshire, southern Maine, and northeast Massachusetts.

A Very Grave Matter; http://www.gravematter.com/

New Hampshire Cemeteries List - If you're not sure which county your ancestor is buried in, or the name of the cemetery within the county, this website provides a by county listing of cemeteries in Ne Hampshire.

New Hampshire Cemeteries List
http://www.epodunk.com/counties/nh_county.html

Political Graveyard - contains a Geographical Index to cemeteries in New Hampshire where politicians have been buried.

Political Graveyard; http://politicalgraveyard.com/geo/NH/cem-index.html

New Hampshire Obituaries

Obituaries can reveal a wealth about our ancestor and other relatives. You can search our **New Hampshire Newspaper Obituaries Listings** from hundreds of New Hampshire newspapers online for free.

New Hampshire Newspaper Obituaries Listings:
http://obituarieshelp.org/new_hampshire_newspaper_obituaries.html

New Hampshire Wills and Probate Records

Court records are an excellent resource for locating ancestors in New Hampshire. It is possible that they may be listed as plaintiffs, defendants, witnesses, or jurors, and there are many types of cases they could have been involved in such as; law suits, property disputes, adoption, divorce, debt settlements, and many other matters. The value in court records is that they can establish relationships between family members, reveal places of residence, occupations, personal descriptions, and more. Following are some excellent resources for New Hampshire probate records.

New England Historic Genealogical Society – early New Hampshire probate records on microfilm.

New England Historic Genealogical Society: http://www.americanancestors.org/home.html

New Hampshire State Archives – probate records of the Superior Court (marriage, divorce, alimony, equity and appeals) 1769 – Present, Court of Common Pleas (civil matters) 1769 – 1859 and those of County Courts 1771 – 1920.

New Hampshire State Archives: http://sos.nh.gov/Arch_Rec_Mgmt.aspx

New Hampshire Immigration and Naturalization Records

The early settlers of New Hampshire were originally emigrants from England, Scotland, and Ireland, who were later joined by many French born immigrants from Canada, and subsequently Germany, Poland, Sweden, Greece, and other countries.

The major port of entry for those coming to New England was Boston, and consequently the **Massachusetts State Archives** may have information on your New Hampshire ancestor in their collection of Boston passenger lists for 1848 to 1891.

Massachusetts State Archives:
http://www.sec.state.ma.us/arc/arcgen/genidx.htm

Many Irish emigrants arrived during the period of the Great Famine, and there is a database of close to 700,000 names of Irish who arrived in the USA between 1846 and1851. Many of those emigrants found their way to New Hampshire.
The **Irish Immigrant Database** may also prove useful to genealogists conducting research in New Hampshire. It is a collection of missing persons or information wanted ads published in the Boston Pilot newspaper between 1831 and 1921.

Irish Immigrant Database; http://infowanted.bc.edu/

There is also a **Scottish Emigration Database** maintained by the University of Aberdeen that may prove useful to anyone searching New Hampshire ancestors. It currently identifies over 21,000 Scottish emigrants who left the ports of Glasgow, Greenock and other Scottish ports between 1890 and 1960.

Scottish Emigration Database: http://www.abdn.ac.uk/emigration/

Most New Hampshire naturalization records created prior to 1906 have been microfilmed by the LDS church and are available through their Family History Centers. Many others have also been indexed or transcribed for publication and can be found at local and regional libraries and genealogical and historical societies.

Records held in the New Hampshire State and the US National Archives will include records of Passport Applications, Citizenship Certificates, Declarations of Intent, Alien Registrations, and First Papers.

Native American Records

Access Genealogy – New Hampshire Native American census records, tribal histories, and much more

Access Genealogy: http://www.accessgenealogy.com/new-hampshire-genealogy/

Records of the Bureau of Indian Affairs (BIA)

Records of the Bureau of Indian Affairs (BIA): http://www.archives.gov/research/guide-fed-records/groups/075.html

American Indians Records Repository - records dating from the 1700s including trust, education and other historic Indian Affairs records

American Indian Records Repository
Meritex Enterprises
17501 West 98th Street
Lenexa, KS 66219
Phone: 913-888-0601

American Indians Records Repository: http://www.doi.gov/ost/records_mgmt/american-indian-records-repository.cfm

Missing Matriarchs – Resources for Researching Female New Hampshire Ancestors

Looking for female ancestors requires an adjustment of how we view traditional records sources. A woman's identity was often under that of her husband, and often individual records for them can be difficult to locate. The following resources are effective in locating female ancestors in New Hampshire where traditional records may not reveal them.

Marriage and Divorce Records

The State Department of Health in Concord has the following indexes of marriages and divorces from county to state level on microfilm that can be very useful for finding female ancestors.

1. Grafton County Supreme Court equity records 1881-1918 (film 1763365 ff.)
2. Grafton County Supreme Court of Judicature court records, 1774-1821, 1836-1837, court dockets 1774-1819, 1833-1851 (film 1763455 ff.)
3. Index to divorces and annulments pre-1938 (film 1001323 ff.)
4. Marriage Index, colonial era to 1900 (film 1001120 ff.)
5. Bride's Index, 1640-1900 (film 0975678 ff.)

Bibliographies

1. *Index of References to American Women in Colonial Newspapers Through 1800*, Helen F. Evans (The Bibliographer, 1979)
2. *Hands That Built New Hampshire: Spinning and Weaving in New Hampshire,* Federal Writer's Project
3. *A History of the New Hampshire Federation of Women's Clubs, 1895-1940,* Alice Stratton Harriman (Musgrave Printing House, 1941)
4. *The Paved Way: A History of New Hampshire Women,* Olive Tardiff (Women for Weekly Publishing, 1980)

Selected Resources for New Hampshire Women's History

Diamond Library
University of New Hampshire
Durham, NH 03824

Special Collections
Baker Library
Dartmouth College
Hanover, NH 03755

Common New Hampshire Surnames

The following surnames are among the most common in New Hampshire and are also being currently researched by other genealogists. If you find your surname here, there is a chance that some research has already been performed on your ancestor.

Adams, Allen, Angles, Arris, Ashcroft, Atkins, Baldwin, Barnes, Bartlett, Bean, Beckett, Beers, Bellemore, Bergeron, Blake, Blunt, Bond, Bonney, Botting, Bourne, Brody, Brown, Bruce, Burleigh, Burns, Campbell, Carr, Carson, Chandler, Chase, Chickering, Childs, Church, Cilley, Clark, Clayton, Clough, Coffin, Conger, Conner, Cote, Craig, Currier, Cusick, Davis, Dayton, Dean, Dewan, Dolloff, Dow, Downing, Drew, Dreyerwicz, Dudley, Dunn, Dunne, Durant, Durgin, Eaton, Ellis, Fellowes, Fellows, Ferland, Fisher, Fletcher, Florence, Fogg, Ford, Fowler, Fox, Freese, French, Gardner, Garland, Gile, Gilman, Godfrey, Goodhue, Gordon, Graves, Greeley, Green, Groulx, Hall, Harrington, Hartwell, Hersey, Hill, Hoitt, Holcomb, Howe, Hubbard, Hurd, Hussey, Hutchins, Jewett, Jones, Judd, Judkins, Kemp, King, Kinney, Kuykendall, Kwit, LaBelle, LaBreque, Ladd, Laflin, Landry, Lang, Larrabee, LaVoy, Lawrence, Leavitt, Legat, Leighton, Libby, Locke, Lombardo, Louger, Louridas, Lyford, lynch, Lyon, MacIntosh, Marquis, Marshall, Marston, Martin, Mataragas, McGall, McNamara, Merrill, Mettler, Miles, Moore, Moreau, Morin, Morrill, Moses, Munn, Murch, Neal, Nichols, O'Neil, Ouellette, Overlock, Page, Painter, Palmer, Paquette, Parenteau, Parsons, Patterson, Paul, Payson, Peasons, Peterson, Philbrick, Phillips, Picard, Piper, Porter, Prentice, Prescott, Pryor, Quinn, Rafford, Rand, Rawlins, Reardon, Richardson, Ricker, Robbins, Robinson, Rollins, Rolston, Ross, Rowe, Rowley, Rundlett, Russell, Safford, Sanborn, Scribner, Severance, Shaw, Sherburne, Shipley, Shola, Sholler, Shurburn, Simpson, Sinclair, Slodzinski, Small, Smith, Steen, Stevens, Strandell, Taylor, Tennant, Thibodeau, Thomas, Thyng, Tibbetts, Tilton, Todorovich, Trafton, Trask, Tucker, Varney, Veasey, Vinyard, Wales, Wangberg, Ward, Warner, Watson, Weidle, West, Whipple, White, Wiggin, Winship, Woodworth, Wyman, Yeaton, York

About the Author

Gary L. Morris worked from 2009 to 2014 as a professional researcher for a major player in the genealogy field. After tracing his family lineage back to 1683, he has decided to publish these helpful guides to share the valuable information he has discovered during his career to help others trace their family lineages. An avid genealogist himself, he hopes you will find this guide factual, thorough, helpful, and most of all, effective in helping you to find your family members.